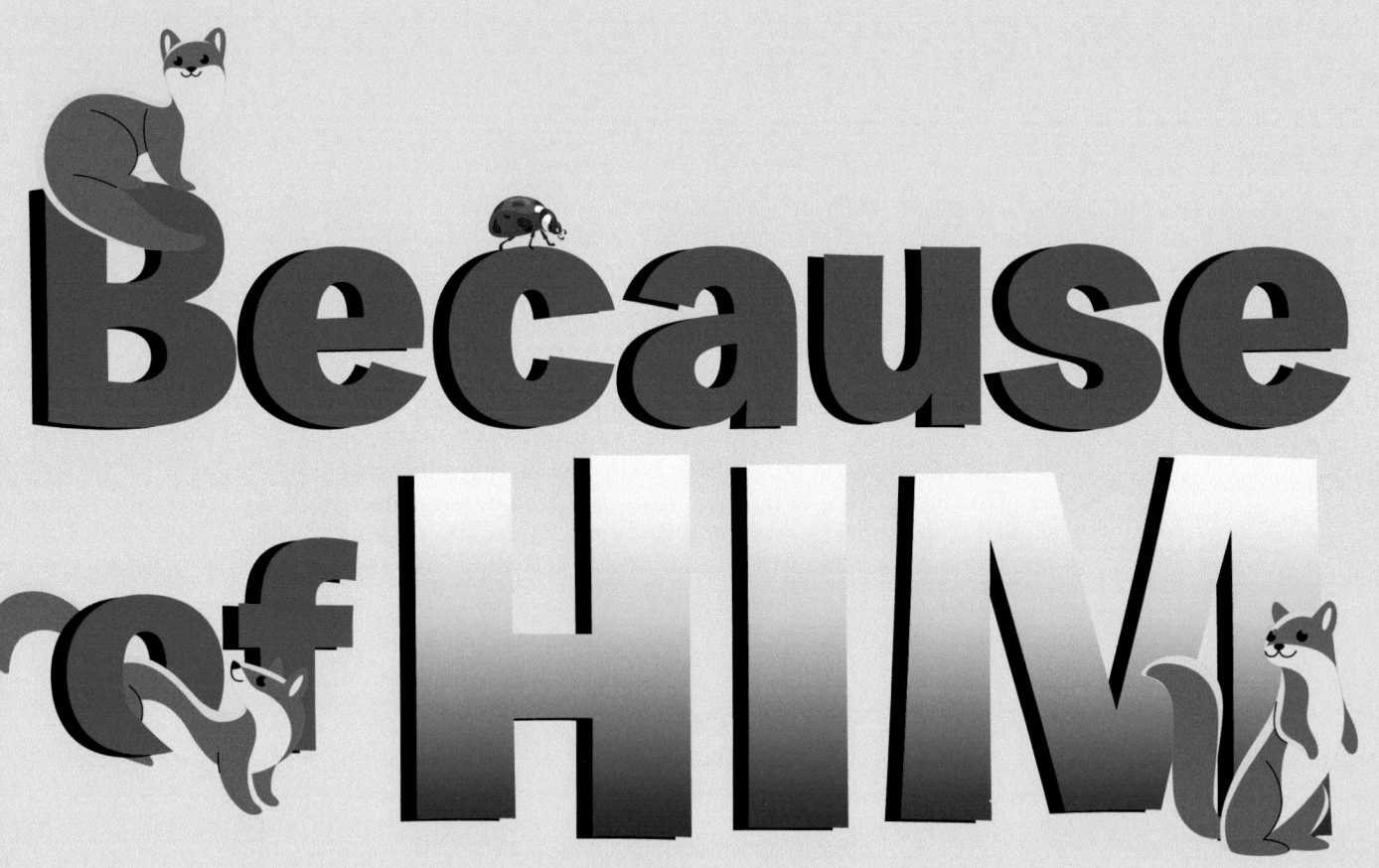

Because of HIM

NO Child is Fatherless

KIMBERLY RIPPBERGER

Illustrations by Mike Motz

To order additional copies of this book, contact:
Xlibris
844-714-8691
www.Xlibris.com
Orders@Xlibris.com

ISBN: 978-1-6641-7120-6 (sc)
ISBN: 978-1-6641-7119-0 (e)

Library of Congress Control Number: 2021908364

Print information available on the last page

Rev. date: 04/27/2021

To my children, you are my everything. Thank you for your never-ending love and grace.

"Come on, kids! We have to get ready for church," Momma exclaims as she searches the living room, looking for Glen.

Oliver quietly whispers, "I found him, Momma." He then pounces on Glen, surprising his furry buddy who jumps right into his arms. "Come on, Glen," says Oliver. "I got to get ready to go!"

Momma, Mia, Bella, Harper, and Oliver all drive off to church. Little did Momma know that Glen had sneaked into the car. He was not going to be left behind.

"Sit down, class, so that I can tell you about the cake-decorating contest." Mrs. C explained, "Because it is Fathers' Day, your fathers are going to help you with all the preparations."

The class giggled with excitement.

"This time moms are not allowed to help in any way," Mrs. C continued with a smile.

"Okay, class, we need to start on our lessons." Mrs. C then began to tell them about Jesus as the class listened intently.

"I want to make a cake that looks like a ladybug. They are just so cute," said Harper.

"I want to make a cake with chocolate, a pizza, a cheeseburger, some gummy worms, and oh, yummy," Oliver said while licking his lips.

"I want to make a cake that looks just like these shoes! Aren't they the cutest?" Bella exclaims as she shows off her fancy cheetah-print shoes.

Mia twirls happily as she exclaims, "I want to make a hot pink cake with sparkles just like my new purse!" Her twirling stops abruptly as she sees who is hiding in her brand-new purse. "Glen, get out of my purse!" Mia squeals.

"Momma, what are we going to do?" a teary-eyed Mia asks. "We don't have a father to help us."

"Does that mean we can't be in the contest?" asks Oliver.

"Oh, but you do!" Momma says. "Come over here and sit down. I want to read to you something from God's Word."

Bella got Momma's Bible from the coffee table, and they all piled up on the couch.

"It says in Psalm 68 that God is the 'Father to the fatherless.' Do you know why that is included in the Bible?" Momma asks her children.

Harper thinks she knows the answer. However, when all eyes turn to her, she just shakes her head no.

"All right then," Momma says. "God included that because He wants each of you to know just how very special you are to Him and how much He loves you. He watches over each of you, and He will never leave you. One of the ways that God, our Father, watches over us is by placing family and friends into our lives. Come, let's see if Grandpa can help," Momma concludes as they all get up to go see Grandpa.

"Grandpa, Grandpa, can you help us make a cake for our Sunday school contest?" asks Oliver as he runs toward Grandpa. "We put our names into a cup for you to pick," he says as he hands Grandpa the mug.

"Grandma, Glen picked my ladybug cake!" Harper exclaims as she jumps up and down with excitement. "Thank you, Glen." Glen begins to get what looks like a smile on his face as Harper continues to pet him. This made all the kids laugh.

"Okay, kiddos, bring in the stuff," Momma directs.

DRAW A PICTURE OF GLEN SMILING BELOW-

"Look, Grandma, look what we made," Bella says as she proudly holds up their beautiful ladybug cake. "We are going to win for sure!" she exclaims as she examines the marvelous piece of work in her hands.

Momma looks at her incredible family: her mother, her father, her three beautiful girls, and the crazy-haired son that God has blessed her with. She even thanks God for Glen. Her heart is incredibly full of love.

"Let's put our cake right here in the middle of all the other cakes," orders Mia.

"Look at this cake—it is so tall," says Bella as she surveys the tables full of interesting cakes.

Mia and Bella are talking so quickly and in such high voices that there is no hiding their excitement.

Harper says in her quietest and tiniest voice possible, "And this one is so small."

"This cake has a lot of frosting," says Oliver as he licks his lips.

"And this one has none," says Grandpa as he looks at his four beautiful grandkids and thanks God for His blessings.

"Glen! Oh no, Glen, get off there!" Oliver yells as he sees that Glen is just about to knock over an entire table of cakes.

"We are the winners, yay!" Bella squeals with excitement as she sees the judges placing the trophy right in front of their cake.

"Can we eat our cake, Grandpa?" Mia asks.

"Okay," says Grandpa. "But then I need to get you home. We have had a very long day."

"Let's say our prayers and get into bed," says Momma.

"Dear God, thank You for Glen," prays Oliver as he sees Glen sneaking under his bed. "And for Grandpa and Grandma and that we won! Oh, and thank You, God, because You made us a family . . . Momma, when do you think I can get a new guitar, huh, Momma?"

Momma kisses Oliver's forehead and tells him good night.

"Thank You, God, that You are our Father and that You gave us our family," prays Mia as she looks at the picture of her family by her bed. "I cannot wait until I am a mommy just like you," says Mia as she hugs her mom even tighter.

"Thank You for Grandma and Grandpa, for Mia, Harper, and Oliver, and even Glen," prays Bella, yawning with exhaustion. "Oh, and Mommy. I love you, Momma."

"Thank You for cake and for pizza and for my sisters and brother. I am still hungry!" says Harper as she licks her lips, again thinking about all those yummy cakes.

Momma kisses each of her girls and tucks them into their beds.

"My Heavenly Father, thank You for these three blue-eyed girls and my crazy-haired boy. Thank You for the way that You watch over us, that You love us and protect us. Thank You for the many ways You have blessed us," prays Momma.

Can you draw a picture of your family so that we can include your family with ours? Oh, and do not forget to include your pets. Glen is always looking for someone to play with.

Because of Him

No child is fatherless.

Do not fear, for He is with you.

You can do all things through Christ.

Nothing can separate us from the love of God.

He will strengthen you and help you.

God will meet all your needs according to the riches of His glory in Christ Jesus.

Encouragement to the reader